"All over this nation, God is stirring the hearts of men to rise up and enter into their God-given destiny. Lou Turner's lifelong passion is to see men enter into their divine purpose in life. 'Living Life God's Way,' of which this book is a part, is born out of this passion. Throughout this Bible study series, Turner opens up God's Word to help you discover HIS plan for your success in your life, family, and work. If you are ready to get off the treadmill, to begin to enjoy God's fullness in your life and make a significant contribution to the world around you, I recommend that you dive into this life-transforming Bible study."

Hal H. Sacks, D.Min., *BridgeBuilders International Leadership Network*

"It seems North American culture is rapidly moving toward what the Bible calls 'everyone doing what is right in his own mind' (Judges 21:25). The prophet Isaiah declared, 'Woe to those who call evil, good, and good, evil' (Isaiah 5:20). This Bible study series will challenge every man in the 21st century as 'iron sharpens iron'! The Q&As at the end of each chapter really personalize the teaching."

Dennis Conner, *Co-Founder/President, Called to Serve Prayer-Coaching Ministry*

"I have known Lou Turner for over twenty years. Lou loves Jesus and has built his life on the Word of God. Lou's Bible study series, 'Living Life God's Way,' is full of biblical truth that has been tested and can be applied by disciples of Jesus in practical ways. These books will help you grow in your faith and gain confidence and competence, which will increase your fruitfulness in Christ.

Mark Buckley, *Founding Pastor of Living Streams Church*

Living Life God's Way

Repentance, Forgiveness, and Restitution

Lou Turner

Repentance, Forgiveness, and Restitution
First Edition, 2020
Copyright © 2020 by Lou Turner

Repentance, Forgiveness, and Restitution is part of the Living Life God's Way Series by Lou Turner.

All rights reserved. No part of this publication may be reproduced, stored in a retrieval system, or transmitted in any form by any means—electronic, mechanical, photocopy, recording, or otherwise—except for brief quotations in critical reviews or articles, without the prior permission of the publisher, except as provided by U.S. copyright law.

Unless otherwise marked, Scriptures are taken from the ESV® Bible (The Holy Bible, English Standard Version®) copyright © 2001 by Crossway Bibles, a publishing ministry of Good News Publishers. ESV Text Edition: 2016. The ESV® text has been reproduced in cooperation with and by permission of Good News Publishers. Unauthorized reproduction of this publication is prohibited. All rights reserved.

Scriptures marked NIV are taken from the Holy Bible, New International Version®, NIV®. Copyright © 1973, 1978, 1984, 2011 by Biblica, Inc.™ Used by permission of Zondervan. All rights reserved worldwide. www.zondervan.com The "NIV" and "New International Version" are trademarks registered in the United States Patent and Trademark Office by Biblica, Inc.™

Scriptures marked TLB are taken from *The Living Bible*, copyright © 1971. Used by permission of Tyndale House Publishers, Inc., Carol Stream, Illinois 60188. All rights reserved.

Some of the anecdotal illustrations in this book are true to life and are included with the permission of the persons involved. All other illustrations are composites of real situations, and any resemblance to people living or dead is coincidental.

To order additional books:
www.amazon.com
www.hislifeinus.com

ISBN: 978-1-7331186-6-8

Editorial and Book Packaging: Inspira Literary Solutions, Gig Harbor, WA
Book Design: PerfecType, Nashville, TN
Cover Design: MTWdesign, Dickson, TN
Printed in the USA by Ingram Spark

He will be like a tree firmly planted by streams of water,
Which yields its fruit in its season
And its leaf does not wither;
And in whatever he does, he prospers.

Psalm 1:3

TABLE OF CONTENTS

Preface   ix

How to Use This Book   xi

Introduction   xiii

1. The Importance of Forgiving   1

2. Forgiveness Where It Hurts   13

3. Asking Forgiveness and Making Restitution   25

A Final Word   41

About the Author   43

PREFACE

We live in a world that has largely forgotten what manhood is about. In the Western world, men are often portrayed on television as buffoons who are out of touch and must rely on their wives to straighten them out. These characters are portrayed as silly, insensitive, lacking common sense, and when they do speak, they are generally wrong. They are generally portrayed as either ridiculously weak or overly macho. They are not able to commit to a long-term relationship and generally mistreat women. Positive role models are hard to find in the media.

However, the Bible teaches a different type of manhood, the authentic one. Men are to be leaders, loving their wives and children, excelling in their work, and standing for truth. They are to be men of wisdom, knowledge, having godly character and seeking after God and His direction. They are to be exhibiting godly leadership at church, in the community, and in business, and to be a light to those around them. They are to be men of compassion and love, as well as courageous and bold when needed.

Men go astray from these ideals, including Christian men, due to improper convictions or beliefs about life. They have received these from various sources: well-meaning family and friends, the media, and the culture around them—a world system that promotes the tearing down of God's biblical truths.

But without proper biblical foundation, we will all go astray.

PREFACE

That's why I wrote these books, containing insights, observations, and biblical truths distilled over the course of my decades of life and ministry. Each section is designed to be a stand-alone section for study and consideration. I hope this series, *Living Life God's Way*, will be used to disciple men in biblical truths for life. Whether you use it for yourself, with a group, or to mentor or disciple someone else, my hope is that it will be a blessing to you and encourage you to seek God and grow in Him.

HOW TO USE THIS BOOK

What does it mean to be a "good" husband and father?
How do I live out the Christian life at work?
What does God want from me—and how am I supposed to find that out?

These were questions that plagued me as a young man—questions, I learned, that are at the front of many men's minds at various times in their lives. For me, these questions began my quest to seek God and discover the answers, and my discoveries, over the years of my life, led to this series of booklets, *Living Life God's Way*. The series discusses 13 topics that every man must deal with, regardless of his work, calling, profession, or circumstances. It is difficult to know how to live the Christian life without understanding what God says about these areas of life.

These topics are:

1. Seeking and Finding God
2. Who You Are in Christ
3. A Man's Work and Ministry
4. Understanding Authority
5. A Man and His Wife
6. A Man and His Children
7. Getting Guidance from God

HOW TO USE THIS BOOK

8. Overcoming Strongholds
9. A Man and Money
10. Repentance, Forgiveness, and Restitution
11. Being a Leader
12. A Man and Sex
13. The Test of Pride

You can use these books to study on your own, in a small group, or with a larger group of men. Each topic or booklet is a stand-alone study, and a person can begin with any one he chooses. They are different lengths and can be adapted to various settings—home, church, or community—all topics that are pertinent to today. They can all be found and purchased at www.hislifeinus.com, or on Amazon.com.

Explore what the Bible says about these important and critical areas. The encouragement is to read these with an open heart, asking God to reveal His truth to you in each of these areas of life. Pray that His Spirit will show you His truth, so that you may live in it and enjoy all God has for you. I pray that you experience the blessing and presence of God in your life as you draw closer to Him and more aware of His leading in every area of your life.

INTRODUCTION TO REPENTANCE, FORGIVENESS, AND RESTITUTION

Forgiveness, along with repentance and restitution, is of vital importance to our spiritual health. Simply due to the nature of life itself, as well as our interactions with others throughout our lifetime, we are bound to experience misunderstandings, hurt, and offenses that we will need to forgive. Sadly, many people are physically or spiritually sick because they haven't forgiven others.

Jesus addressed forgiveness on more than one occasion. When He did, there was no beating around the bush. He discussed it in plain and forthright terms we can all understand. Knowing it was important to Him should make it important to us, too. After all, it leads to great freedom, healing, and a deeper experience of God's grace and forgiveness toward us! With all that in mind, let's look at this crucial area of life.

Chapter 1

The Importance of Forgiving

Steve was brought up in a Christian home. Both of his parents had a genuine zeal for God, and his growing up years centered around the home and church attendance. But a deep relationship never developed between him and his dad. His father was so involved in church activities that there was little time for Steve. In fact, his dad had been told, "Put God first, and He will take care of your family." In other words, you don't have to spend a lot of time with your family. If you prioritize the Lord's work, all will be well. Unfortunately, Steve's father took this advice very much to heart.

Many pastors and Christian workers have bought into that line of thought, only to lose relationship with their spouses and children. Sometimes this results in them losing their families literally, through divorce or alienation. The same can be true of a father who is a workaholic. He loves his work and succeeds there, but he loses his family and fails in one of the most important arenas of his life.

Steve's dad also had a real problem with anger. He wanted Steve to be a model child, so the family reputation would not be tarnished in the church. He would get angry when Steve didn't live up to his expectations. Steve was afraid of his father and grew up trying to avoid him. This created insecurity in his family relationships, and in other relationships as he grew older.

As Steve grew older and began to seek God for himself, he realized how much hurt, disappointment, anger, and fear were in his life. He tried to overcome these problems, determined he would not be like his father. But he was still bothered by the effects of these problems in his life. At times he felt anger and a deep-seated resentment of his parents. Inside, he felt inadequate and insecure. He realized he felt rejected and unloved and needed God to heal his inner man. He had been stuck and mired in this pattern for most of his life. He realized he was not experiencing the joy in his life he should as a Christian. He wanted and needed peace and freedom.

On the positive side, Steve sought God, ministered to others, loved his family, and was blessed by God in many ways. But inside, he was not completely whole, and this troubled him deeply.

As he processed these things, Steve also came to realize he had trouble trusting God. Since God was his ultimate Father, and he did not have a loving relationship with his earthly father, he had trouble believing God loved him, accepted him just as he was, and valued him. Steve knew he needed a breakthrough.

While studying what 1 Corinthians 13 says about love, Steve realized he didn't love his parents as he should; his feelings toward them were full of conflict. He desired resolution and relationship, but felt awkward about how to move forward. Then, one Sunday, his pastor preached on forgiveness. Steve saw that the key to healing in his life lay in forgiving his parents. Steve was certainly not perfect and had made many mistakes growing up. But inside he knew he needed spiritual and emotional healing—and the place to start was with forgiving his parents, particularly his father.

Steve's true experience has been repeated countless times in countless variations. Like Steve, many men have been deeply hurt and feel rejected. Most men do not know how to show love and proper affection to their children, as most of them did not receive that from their father. Some men have been abused either physically or emotionally. This brings feelings of deep disappointment, hurt, and rejection, along with fear and anger.

Most young boys that have been physically or emotionally abused carry that with them into adulthood, often trying to hide it. They respond to the hurt and rejection with anger, bitterness, insecurity, or even a desire for revenge. All of these types of emotions get bottled up inside and can wreak havoc in our lives. They can be like a poison that spreads its toxin.

As Steve began to realize, forgiveness releases the hurt in our hearts and minds and healing begins. The wound gets cleansed and now can begin to heal. Often, those that have hurt us do not realize it and did not intent to do so. Forgiveness brings release and starts the healing process. We release those who we feel hurt us to God, and choose to reject the need to make them pay for the wrong they have done us. When we make this transition, our hearts are freed from the effects of the emotions we have been harboring.

Forgiveness does not erase the pain others have caused us, nor does it make what they have done to us "okay." What it does do is release us from the toxin of unforgiveness that has spread into our lives as a result. It allows healing to replace pain and brings the ability to experience love where we have experienced rejection. It frees us so we can begin to experience joy and peace. God's love will heal the pain, hurts, and rejection and replace them with peace, joy, and a feeling of being accepted and valued by God.

Many fathers come from an upbringing in which their fathers did not show them love, and therefore they did not learn how to love their sons by example. Many men were taught they need their sons to be "tough" and therefore thought showing them love, grace, and kindness would only make them weak. But there is a great difference between weakness and meekness; between showing love and trying to force someone to be strong or manly. A man who is whole can show vulnerability and be kind and merciful, and still have great courage and boldness when needed. Jesus did. He showed unending kindness to those who needed grace, forgiveness, and love. He also showed great courage and boldness when he spoke out the truth and stood against those who were leading others astray. He is our example.

Forgiveness Starts with Us

We have to view unforgiveness as a poison that prevents us from experiencing all God has for us. If we don't get rid of it, the poison will spread and contaminate us. It will affect our relationships with others and with God.

In Matthew 18:21, Peter asked Jesus, "Lord, how often shall my brother sin against me, and I forgive him? Up to seven times?" Obviously, Peter thought forgiving someone seven times was quite a lot. He probably thought that was being very generous. Jesus' response must have been quite a surprise.

"I do not say to you, up to seven times," Jesus replied, "but up to seventy times seven" (18:22). Jesus said to forgive and then continue to forgive. We are to live in forgiveness, guarding our hearts and lives from unforgiveness. Peter had to realize that forgiveness was first for him, and then for the one being forgiven.

Harboring hurt or anger will take its toll on us. Unforgiveness can bring discord, discontent, a critical spirit, gossip, and even physical problems. These seeds, when sown into relationships and organizations, weaken them. Unforgiveness robs us of peace and steals our joy. It can affect our relationships with others, including our wives, children, and friends.

Lack of forgiveness will not render us completely ineffective or useless to God. Neither will it make us unable to experience relationship with Him and others. But all of our relationships, including our relationship with God, will be adversely affected if we harbor unforgiveness. Jesus knew this and was trying to teach Peter the critical importance of living in forgiveness.

Forgiveness Is Crucial

After Jesus' statement to Peter, He told a parable about forgiving and showing mercy, a story found in Matthew 18:23-35. In this account, a man owed a king a great deal of money: 10,000 talents. A talent was equal to 75 pounds, which means this was a great fortune. Imagine what 750,000 pounds (10,000 x 75 pounds) of silver or gold would be worth in any era! The man threw himself at the king's mercy. In that day, a person could be sold into slavery, along with his family, in order to work off debt. This man was facing such a fate. However, the king was moved by his appeal and forgave him the debt.

Jesus was making a point here. More than likely, this parable was a fictional story to teach a practical lesson. The amount of money owed by the first man was huge, more than probably could ever be paid back. That was the point. A huge debt that could not be repaid was forgiven, just like our debt of sin cannot be paid back by our efforts. It is God's love and grace and the provision of Jesus on the cross that wipe away our debt. His graciousness and love, not our work or effort, put us in right standing with Him.

The story goes on and the man forgiven of the debt then went out and found another man who owed him 100 denarii, about 100 days wages. He demanded the man pay the debt. When the man begged him for more time, he would not grant it but sold the debtor into slavery.

The king found out and angrily called the man he had forgiven to his court. This man had been forgiven such a great debt but could not in turn forgive another! The king threw the man into prison.

Then Jesus said, "So also my heavenly Father will do to every one of you, if you do not forgive your brother from your heart" (verse 35). Wow, what a statement! Can Jesus really mean this? The answer lies in the importance God places on relationships. Jesus is making a point here. In this parable, Jesus was showing that the one man owed a fortune and was forgiven the debt. The amount of money he was forgiven was almost unthinkable. It was huge. Who would do such a thing? Jesus did this for all of us. He was showing that anything could be forgiven, no matter how great.

While we may not literally go to prison, we can live in a prison of unforgiveness and have to endure the effects it brings into our lives. Our unforgiveness keeps God from healing us in those areas where we are affected by it. That's what Jesus meant. He was emphasizing that the impact of unforgiveness on our lives is a heavy price to pay.

Scripture's Emphasis on Relationship

In Scripture, God puts a great deal of importance in relationships. Unity—in the church, in the home, in marriage, in friendships, and in the workplace—is critically important. In addition, God wants our relationships with Him to be unhindered. Because of His love for us, God desires relationship with us and wants us to have the privilege of being a part of His plan here on Earth. He wants us to walk in the power of His Spirit and to live out His best in our lives. It can be difficult to do this fully, if not impossible, if we are walking in unforgiveness.

Throughout Scripture, we see passage after passage demonstrating that God not only wants our hearts to be right with Him, but also with others:

God warned of judgment for how the nation of Israel treated others. In most of the prophetic messages where God warned Israel of coming judgment, He told them that if they would repent and begin to treat others fairly, with justice and mercy, He would relent of the judgment. We find an example in Amos 2:6-8, which says,

> *This is what the LORD says; for three sins of Israel, even for four, I will not turn back my wrath. They sell the righteous for silver, and the needy for a pair of sandals. They trample on the heads of the poor as upon the dust of the ground and deny justice to the oppressed. Father and son use the same girl and so profane my holy name.*

The prophets continually spoke to Israel of how they had turned away from God and how they were treating others. It was twofold: their relationship with God and their relationship and treatment of others.

God's greatest command is that we love. Matthew records that an expert in Jewish law asked Jesus, "Teacher, which is the greatest commandment in the Law?"

Jesus replied,

> *"Love the Lord your God with all your heart and with all your soul and with all your mind. This is the first and*

> *greatest commandment. And the second is like it; Love you neighbor as yourself. All the Law and Prophets hang on these two commandments." (Matthew 22:36-40)*

This account is repeated in Luke and John. The Lord wanted us to get the message so it is stated three times. (Anytime the Bible stresses something more than once, we need to pay extra attention!)

Think about it: ***All of the law and prophecies of the prophets hang on those two commandments; loving God and loving others.*** That's the core teaching of the Bible! That's what Jesus came to teach us and show us! God looks upon our hearts toward Him, and our attitudes and actions toward others.

Reconciliation is God's will. Romans 12:17-21 gives detailed instructions regarding how we are to respond to someone who does evil to us:

> *Do not repay anyone evil for evil. Be careful to do what is right in the eyes of everybody. If it is possible,* ***as far as it depends on you****, live at peace with everyone. Do not take revenge, my friends, but leave room for God's wrath, for it is written: 'It is mine to avenge; I will repay', says the Lord. If your enemy is hungry, feed him; if he is thirsty, give him something to drink. In doing this, you will heap burning coals on his head. Do not be overcome by evil, but overcome evil with good. (emphasis mine)*

Others may not forgive, but we must, both for our sakes and for the sake of re-establishing relationship. Others may not ever seek to reconcile, but we must, for it is our Father's will that we try to do so.

Forgiveness is part of Jesus' model prayer. Jesus continued this trend of thought in Matthew 6:5-15 as He gave a model prayer. At the end of the prayer, He said, *"For if you forgive men their trespasses, your heavenly Father will also forgive you. But if you* *do not forgive men their trespasses, neither will your Father forgive your trespasses."* That was the second time Jesus stated this. So to God, forgiveness is ***very*** important.

When we accept Jesus as our Savior, we are forgiven all our sins. But unforgiveness can cause some of the effects of sin to hang onto us. We are saved and forgiven, but the Father's healing and forgiveness may not be experienced in the areas where we harbor unforgiveness.

Jesus' entire purpose was reconciliation. Jesus certainly modeled this Himself. Even on the cross, after being beaten mercilessly and suffering the shame and excruciating pain of crucifixion, He cried out, "Father forgive them, for they do not know what they are doing" (Luke 23:34, NIV).

In His pain and suffering, He chose to forgive. He was giving His life for others and He did not want it to be in vain; He wanted to reconcile the world to God. He wants our lives to be a part of His purpose—reconciling, or leading, others to Him. We do this by our words and deeds.

Forgiveness is central to being complete followers of God. In the Sermon on the Mount, Jesus taught,

> *You have heard that it was said, "Love your neighbor and hate your enemy." But I tell you; Love your enemies and pray for those who persecute you, that you may be sons of your Father in heaven. He causes His sun to rise on the evil and the good, and sends rain on the righteous and the unrighteous. If you love those who love you, what reward will you get? Are not even the tax collectors doing that? And if you greet only your brothers, what are you doing more than others? Do not even pagans do that? Be perfect, therefore, as your heavenly Father is perfect. (Matthew 5:43-48)*

The word used for "perfect" in this passage is the Greek word *teleios,* meaning to be complete or mature. Jesus is saying, "Be complete, be mature; love and forgive others."

Freed through Forgiveness

Our Father's whole heart is to love and reconcile; therefore, in order to be like Him, we are to love others and reconcile with them as well.

After Steve heard his pastor speak about forgiveness, he began to ask God to help him forgive his parents, particularly his dad. He asked God to give him a love for his parents and the ability to move forward with his life. In Steve's case, his dad loved him but did not know how to express it. His dad's anger had hurt Steve and had caused deep feelings of rejection.

Over time, Steve's relationship with his parents improved. But more importantly, the way he felt about them changed. It began with forgiving his dad and then purposing to love and pray for him.

Steve came to realize his father did love him and had done what he thought was right. His dad had not been taught good parenting skills and did not know how to show love or affection to his children and make them feel valued. It is hard to feel valued when you have grown up not experiencing it. It's also hard to believe God loves and values you if you didn't feel loved when you were growing up.

Releasing others through forgiveness is the first step to beginning the process of experiencing what we missed in our formative years. We forgive, ask God to heal us, and ask Him to reveal His love for us and how He feels about us. We are valued and precious to Him. Remember, those we are forgiving are also loved by Him. He gave His life for them also.

QUESTIONS FOR REFLECTION AND DISCUSSION

1. Are you aware of any unforgiveness in your heart? If so, against whom? Below, write their names and what you feel their offenses have been toward you.

   _____
   _____
   _____
   _____

2. How has this unforgiveness affected you?

   _____
   _____
   _____
   _____

3. Why would you need to forgive these offenses for your own sake?

   _____
   _____
   _____

   For their sakes?

   _____
   _____
   _____

REPENTANCE, FORGIVENESS, AND RESTITUTION

4. Are you willing to forgive them? If so, write out your prayer of forgiveness below. (Use the "Take a Knee" prayer below to help you find words, if you need them.)

_____

_____

_____

_____

TAKE A KNEE

Let's kneel before the Lord and pray. If you are unable to kneel physically, then kneel in your heart to Him. *"Father, I do not want to harbor unforgiveness in my life. I give it to you now. I give the person, the circumstances, the hurt, the betrayal, and the unforgiveness to You. Please take it. Forgive me for harboring unforgiveness. Heal me of all of its effects. Give me the grace I need not only to forgive, but also to walk in forgiveness, choosing it every time unforgiveness tries to come back. Give me the ability not only to forgive, but also to pray for the one involved. May Your love flow in me toward my offenders. You love them; help me to seek their good and experience Your love for them. I claim forgiveness, and I claim the freedom You have for me. I am free! You love me, forgive me, and are extending Your grace toward me now."*

Chapter 2

FORGIVENESS WHERE IT HURTS

The family members or other people with whom we grew up had a primary influence on our lives. They are the ones we had to live with, or if friends, chose to interact with. Therefore, though these relationships were intended to bring us joy and fulfillment, for many they brought hurt and disappointment. In many cases, these relationships are where a problem with anger, fear, immorality, or other issues may have begun.

Denise was in her twenties when she accepted Christ as her Savior. She had some serious issues to deal with. Her father and her brothers had all sexually abused her as she was growing up. She was deeply hurt and wounded. This led her to immoral behavior outside of the home as she was growing up. After she was married, her husband knew of her past, yet loved and accepted her.

When she came to Christ, Denise began to try to deal with her torrent of emotions. She battled hurt, fear, rejection, anger, and even hatred. She wanted to be free and experience inner healing and peace regarding her past. Through prayer and counsel, she came to the realization that she must forgive those who had abused her or taken advantage of her.

She prayed and asked God to heal her. She forgave her father, brothers, and others and then began to pray for them. When the time was right, and with wise counsel, she also called her father and brothers and told them she forgave them. The end of this story has not yet been told. However, she was freed of the hurt and pain she carried. Hatred, fear, and anger left her. Her ability to love, be loved, and feel loved all changed.

Many of us carry negative experiences from our past forward into the present. Like Denise, many men have also been sexually molested as young boys, sometimes by a trusted authority figure. Others of us are married to women who have been abused, and must deal with our anger for how our wife's abusers damaged both her and our marriages.

Sometimes the hurt in our families came from an angry or cold father or mother who punished us harshly. And sometimes, *we* might even be the ones who caused the harm. A clear conscience and a pure heart toward these primary relationships is especially important. (We'll talk more in the next chapter about asking for forgiveness when we are the ones in the wrong.) If we harbor negative emotions against our parents, siblings, or others we grew up with, those emotions will have a definite impact on our lives and our interactions with the people around us.

Thankfully, most families are not abusive in the way Denise experienced. Even so, many of us carry negative experiences from our past forward into the present. If we harbor negative emotions against our parents, siblings, or others we grew up with, those emotions will have a definite influence on our lives.

We may not agree with family members all the time, or choose to live our lives as they do. If there was abuse in our history with them, it may be difficult to have an ongoing relationship. However, we need to forgive them, for our sakes and theirs. Being free of negative emotions toward our family members, is a key to healthy living.

One of the Ten Commandments says, "Honor your father and your mother, so that you may live long in the land the LORD your God is giving you" (Exodus 20:12). This commandment is repeated in Deuteronomy 5:16 and in Ephesians 6:2-3. Jesus also states it several times in the Gospels of Matthew, Mark, and Luke. Obviously honoring our parents is of great importance. It is not only the right thing to do, but it has a direct bearing on our spiritual health and welfare. The Bible says to do it so that "you may live long and that it may go well with you" (Deuteronomy 5:16).

Obviously the reason the Bible emphasizes this is because it is important to the health of our inner person, which includes our spiritual health. God does not want us to carry around things that negatively affect us. He wants us to be healed and whole and to be free of anything that is a hindrance in our life.

What Is Rooted in Your Heart?

Think of your heart as the "soil" of your life, where seeds are planted throughout your lifetime that have a great influence on you. Our hearts can be full of love, forgiveness, peace, and the other fruits of the Spirit mentioned in Galatians 5, or they can be full of hurt, hatred, anger, contentiousness, and conflict, allowing bitterness to take root.

Hebrews 12 speaks about a root of bitterness: *"Look after each other so that no one of you will fail to find God's best blessing,"* it says. *"Watch out that no bitterness takes root among you, for as it springs up it causes deep trouble, hurting many in their spiritual lives"* (Hebrews 12:15-16, TLB)

A root of bitterness is something that can form in us, often as we are growing up. It comes from being hurt repeatedly. The hurt may turn to anger and a deep resentment, which causes us to become bitter. That bitter root may surface in many ways. It might show up as a fear of authority or anger toward authority. It may display itself as a deep distrust of the opposite sex, or as a critical or contentious spirit toward others. (Of course, not everyone who displays these symptoms does so because of bitterness.) Bitterness deep in a person's heart will manifest itself one way or another. It will motivate us and eat away at us. It often drives our interactions with others or our goals in life. The Hebrew passage above says that *"as it springs up, it causes deep trouble, hurting many in their spiritual lives."*

A root of bitterness hurts the person who has it—and usually those around them, too. Because they have lived with it for a long time, they accept it. Until the Lord shows them it is there and is harming their lives and their relationships, they continue to live with it.

It is up to us to guard our hearts, as mentioned in Proverbs 4:23: *"Above all else, guard your heart, for it is the wellspring of life."* We must root out things that are harmful that may be in our hearts, and plant good seed. Galatians 5:22-23 describes what grows in a heart with good seed:, *"But the fruit of the Spirit is love, joy, peace, patience, kindness, goodness, faithfulness, gentleness and self-control."*

These traits are "fruit" of God's Spirit being in us. The Holy Spirit wants to manifest these traits in us because they are God's nature and character. If we are not displaying these things, something is wrong. If there is no joy, there is a problem. If there is a lack of gentleness, kindness, or patience, there is a problem. As we walk with the Lord, and yield to His work in our life, these character traits will grow in us.

However, a root of bitterness can put us in a rut, and keep us from growing spiritually as we should. Anger, hurt, a critical or contentious spirit, or deep distrust can rule our lives. Ephesians 4:30-31 tells us to deal with these areas of our hearts:

"And do not grieve the Holy Spirit of God, with whom you were sealed for the day of redemption. Get rid of all bitterness, rage and anger, brawling and slander, along with every form of malice."

Then it goes on to tell us how to treat each other: "Be kind and compassionate to one another, forgiving each other, just as in Christ God forgave you." Forgiveness, the way God forgave us, is the new standard for our relationships. It conquers the negative things in our lives that can hurt us.

The things that are in our heart will bear fruit, or show up in our lives and actions; whether positive or negative. But God can change our hearts and heal us through the power of His Spirit. When we forgive those who have harmed us and ask God to bring healing to our hearts and make us whole, that is just what He desires to do. He wants our hearts to be rich in the truth of His Word, in the indwelling power of His Spirit, and He desires His fruit to come forth through us.

***God desires His Spirit to wash our hearts and souls
with His "fruits" to clean them,
make them whole, and to flow through us.***

What Forgiveness Is Not

When we talk about forgiveness, particularly in difficult areas where we have harbored long-standing hurt from primary relationships, it is also important that we understand what forgiveness is not. Many of us do not understand forgiveness clearly.

Forgiveness does not mean accepting wrongdoing. Sometimes people think that forgiveness means they are overlooking or accepting the wrong that was done to them. Denise, whose story you read earlier, forgave her father and brothers. But that did not mean Denise dismissed or minimized what was done to her. She knew it was wrong. She also did not condone her past immoral behavior. She understood it was sin and had hurt her life. By asking God to forgive her wrong attitudes toward others and her own wrong actions, she obtained freedom. She was able to let go of these negative emotions and replace them with the power of love and forgiveness.

When we forgive others, we do not condone or minimize their wrong actions. In fact, the reason we need to forgive is because the other person *has* done something wrong to us. We forgive for our sakes and hope for the possibility that the other person will repent. As we cover that relationship and past actions with prayer, God's Spirit begins healing us, restoring us, and helps us to see it with a new perspective. Rather than being stuck, we move beyond it to see it from God's perspective of forgiveness and being made whole.

Forgiveness does not mean we offer ourselves up to be harmed again. Forgiveness also does not mean we automatically resume relationship with those who have harmed us as if nothing ever happened. We may not be able to have meaningful relationship with them because of their lifestyles or their continued ability to harm us. But we can be free.

As men, and leaders in our homes, we want our families to be free of hurt, fear, anger, and hatred. We want them to forgive others as needed. But we cannot allow them to be put into compromising situations. As protectors, we should watch over our families and protect them from ungodly or hurtful influences and relationships. We may forgive the flame for burning us, but we do not willfully put our hands back into the flame.

Note: An exception to this would be if God leads someone to consciously put themselves into harm's way, such as for the sake of the gospel. Some are even martyred, but their reward in heaven is great. Corrie Ten Boom, the famous missionary, was imprisoned in a Nazi labor camp for sheltering Jews during World War II. She saw her sister die and others greatly mistreated and killed. She chose to forgive her oppressors. She actually saw some of them come to Christ as she chose to forgive and pray for them. The power of love and forgiveness won them over—and saved her from living in a lifelong prison of bitterness.

Forgiveness is not a one-time act. Forgiveness begins when we choose to forgive, but it doesn't end there. It continues as we continue to choose to forgive any time thoughts enter our mind that could cause us to take up the offense or hurt again.

We forgive and continue to forgive, just as Jesus told Peter to forgive, 70 times seven times. We guard our heart from allowing unforgiveness or hurt to take root again. We do not allow our thoughts to linger on things we have dealt with already. We do not allow hurt and unforgiveness to take root in our heart again. We live in God's forgiveness, and His love and grace. We then allow that to flow in those areas of our heart and soul.

Forgiveness does not mean we are weak in the face of wrong. Some confuse forgiving and showing love with backing down when faced with wrongdoing. Loving others, and even showing mercy, does not mean we are cowards or unwilling to take a stand when necessary.

Our example is God Himself. He is merciful and loving. In fact, the Bible says in 1 John 4:16, "And so, we know and rely on the love God has for us. God is love. Whoever lives in love lives in God, and God in him." **God is *love Himself*.**

Romans 8:38-39 says, "For I am convinced that neither death nor life, neither angels nor demons, neither the present nor the future, not any powers, neither height nor depth, nor anything else in all creation, will be able to separate us from the love of God that is in Christ Jesus our Lord." All love emanates from God.

And yet, when Christ entered the temple, He drove out the money changers and overturned their tables (Matthew 21:12-13). Jesus demonstrated righteous indignation through what some would consider a violent action.

Why? The religious leaders were leading the people astray. Jesus wanted His house to be a house of prayer, but they were making it a den of thieves. In order to show a proper example and to protect the people from false teaching and practice, He was moved to take action. At other times, He rebuked the Pharisees and other religious leaders. He would have no part of hypocrisy and false teaching that were leading God's people astray.

We see here that love protects. Whether someone is trying to harm us or our families, or a ruthless dictator is killing innocent people, at times it is proper to take action to protect others from evil.

Beyond these kinds of violent scenarios, there is a time to stand for what is right. Refusing to take part in wrong, refusing to lie or take part in deception in order to obtain financial gain, admitting when we are wrong—all these are acts of courage and standing for what is right. In this our motivation is love: love of God and wanting to please Him, as well as love of others and wanting to be a godly example.

Love, mercy, humility, boldness, and courage are all godly traits and character qualities. Courage and boldness are not any less godly than the others. As we grow in character and wisdom, these should all flow out of us.

QUESTIONS FOR REFLECTION AND DISCUSSION

1. Do you sense long-standing bitterness in your heart toward a family member, a group of people, or even an organization? If so, list the names below, and add the reason for your bitterness.

   _____

   _____

   _____

   _____

2. What symptoms might this root be causing in your life (such as a critical or contentious nature)? Describe the effects holding onto this root has had in you, in your marriage, your relationships with your children, or your ability to be close and connected with others. Has it caused you not to be able to trust others, or even God?

   _____

   _____

   _____

   _____

REPENTANCE, FORGIVENESS, AND RESTITUTION

3. Would you like to be free of these symptoms? If so, confess this to the Lord and ask His forgiveness. Ask Him to heal you and make you whole. Write out your prayer below.

_____

_____

_____

_____

4. Have you had any of the following misperceptions about forgiveness? Mark any that apply.
   ___ Forgiveness makes me look weak.
   ___ If I forgive, I am saying what was done to me didn't matter.
   ___ If I forgive, the other person gets off with no consequences.
   ___ I can't forgive until I *feel* forgiving.
   ___ I can't forgive until the other person says he/she is sorry.
   ___ I can never forget what happened, therefore I can't forgive.

5. What do you now understand the truth about forgiveness to be? Write the corrected statement below. (If you have difficulty knowing what the true statement is, ask group members for their input.)

_____

_____

_____

_____

TAKE A KNEE

In this time of prayer, we need to search our hearts. We also need to ask God to reveal anything we need to understand about our relationships with others. Let's pray: *"Heavenly Father, if there are things in my life that are controlling me and keeping me from walking the abundant life, please reveal them to me that I might confess them, and so You can heal me in these areas. I do not want to live in any area of sin that is harmful to me or others in my life. If there is a critical spirit or root of bitterness in my life, reveal that to me. Show me why it is there, and who are the ones I need to forgive in order to be free. Thank You, Father, that You desire for me to live in freedom. You desire me to live in peace, love and joy. Thank You for loving me and wanting to heal and restore me."*

"Father, I want to have courage and Your boldness when I need to confront wrong, as well as meekness and humility. I want to be motivated by love and what is right in Your sight. Give me the balance You desire me to have. Teach me to balance humility with boldness and courage. Build Your character in me."

Chapter 3

Asking Forgiveness and Making Restitution

So, what if we are the one who needs to ask forgiveness? Possibly we may not be aware that we have offended or wronged someone and need to ask forgiveness. Of, we may think the other person is more at wrong than we are, and we are waiting for them to start the process of reconciliation. Let's do a short study that may help clarify this.

First, let's look at the concept of sin in the Bible. The word "sin" is used in the Bible 415 times—308 in the Old Testament and 107 in the New Testament. Variations of the word sin (sinful, sinned, sinners, sinning, etc.) are used 340 times in the Bible. It is an important word in the Bible as it describes our condition before accepting Christ as our Savior, as well as talking about wrongdoing (in thought, attitude, or deed) after we become a Christian.

Jesus talked about sin, or wrongdoing, in both our actions and our attitudes. Webster says that sin is "a voluntary departure from following God's revealed will for us (paraphrase). He states that sin is either a voluntary transgression of God's law or will, or the voluntary neglect to obey God's commands or revealed will. We realize we have all sinned and at times commit sin in our current life.

The issue is not whether we fall short at times, but how we handle that when we realize it. As a loving Father, God convicts His children of sin and wrongdoing. He also disciplines us to teach and train us to move into greater relationship with Him. He wants us to have all He has for us, and He wants to reveal to us what that means. Because of this, He is committed, over our entire lifetime, to revealing to us those things that hinder our walk with Him and that keep us from His best for us. He desires to continue to heal us, free us, and love us.

Often, we are not able to understand or "hear" from Him all He wants to say to us or teach us. It may be because we do not spend enough time seeking Him and wanting to hear from Him. He often uses our circumstances and life activities to reveal His truth as we are open to receive it.

When we stray from the path, God's correction (and discipline, when necessary) are not those of an angry father. Rather, God's correction and discipline are designed to teach, train, and reveal His good intentions toward us. Since all God does is from a heart of love, including His discipline, He has a greater good and purpose in all He does in our lives. He will also rebuke us if need be, either to spare us from a harmful direction we are on or to bring us to repentance of our actions that are hurting us or others. God desires our good and is committed to help us discover that.

Proverbs 3:11-12 (NIV) says, *"My son, do not despise the Lord's discipline and do not resent His rebuke, because the Lord disciplines those He loves, as a father the son he delights in."* John 15:1-2 says,

ASKING FORGIVENESS AND MAKING RESTITUTION

"I am the true vine and My Father is the gardener. He cuts off every branch in Me that bears no fruit, while every branch that does bear fruit He trims clean so that it will be even more fruitful."

Here we see that the Lord both disciplines and "prunes" us, like a young sapling, so that we will be more productive or fruitful. His intention is for us to grow and learn during these times.

Discipline is also a test of our commitment to Him, to see if we will abandon our faith or renew it with a deeper commitment. Just as crisis can either destroy a marriage or make it stronger, depending on how it is handled, so crisis or hardship in our life can cause us to doubt God and depart from the faith, or it can strengthen our commitment to our Lord.

When we are disciplined and pruned, we can grow and become stronger. Sadly, during difficult times, or possibly times of God "pruning" us, some lose heart and abandon their faith, and become "shipwrecked," as the Bible puts it (1 Timothy 1:19).

Also during these times of pruning and discipline, the Lord will often reveal to us things in our lives that need to change. He will reveal areas of sin or shortcomings, where we do not live according to Scripture. God's purpose is that we see these problem areas, repent of them, and receive healing and change. The Bible calls this process "sanctification."

An older version of *Webster's Dictionary* defined sanctification as, "The act of God's grace by which the affections of men are purified or alienated from sin and the world, and focused on their relationship with God. It means to purify, cleanse, or make holy, to set apart for God's purpose."* (As a side note, Noah Webster was a godly man who memorized large passages of Scripture. I don't like what they have done to his legacy in current dictionaries

---

* Webster, Noah, *American Dictionary of the English Language*, 1828.

with his name on it. I like this version as it still has much of his original work in it.)

Throughout our lives, the process of sanctification will be taking place. At times, it will be more intense as God works deeply in our hearts to purify us, and draw us closer to Him. During these times, there will be things we will need to repent of.

For example, I know of a man named John who had a significant problem with pride—so much so that it caused others to shy away from him. They liked John, but at times were taken back by his pride.

It was during a time of Bible reading and prayer that the Holy Spirit revealed to John how his pride had affected his relationships with family members. In this moment, John faced a question we all face: What if we come to realize that we have offended, hurt, or harmed others? What if we are the one who needs to be forgiven?

If the Lord shows us that we have been guilty of hurting or offending others, we have a responsibility to God and to them. We are to respond to God's conviction, repent of our wrongdoing, ask God and the person for forgiveness, and follow God's leading regarding making restitution.

John took to heart God's conviction regarding his pride. During a family gathering, he asked if he could address the whole family. He confessed his problem with pride and told them he realized it had affected his relationships with them. He asked their forgiveness. A new bond developed in the family. His willingness to humble himself brought healing into relationships.

Repenting of Wrongdoing

Repentance is a primary and basic doctrine. It is necessary in order to obtain salvation and a right standing before the Lord. However, repentance takes place after salvation as well, as the Lord convicts us of sin or wrongdoing.

From this point forward in this study, I will use the word "wrongdoing" often to refer to "sin." Please understand, my focus is not meant to be on our wrongdoing, but on God and His love and goodness. I am well aware that we don't overcome wrongdoing by focusing on it. We become overcomers by getting more of God in our lives and getting closer to Him! He is our source of power and revelation.

We overcome the power of sin by the power of God. If we focus on our shortcomings and wrongdoings, we will be in bondage to it. If we focus on our relationship with God and drawing closer to Him, we will overcome the power of sin and come into all that God has for us.

Repentance means "to feel pain, sorrow or regret for something we have done or spoken; to change our mind about our conduct, our hearts motives, and purpose to live according to God's standards. It can bring a godly sorrow because we have violated God's Word and thus hurt Him [God], who loves us."* This is not generally the modern understanding of "repentance"; even in the Church, many of us have a lesser view of repentance.

I once counseled a woman, June, who was not happy in her marriage. Her husband did not mistreat her; he wasn't abusive, he wasn't unfaithful. Nor had he abandoned her. She was just not happy with her marriage. In counseling, she told me that if things did not change soon, she was going to divorce her husband and look for someone else. When I told her that was not God's desire and a violation of Scripture, she stated, "I know that. But I will repent afterwards, and God will forgive me." She was serious!

---

* Webster, Noah, *American Dictionary of the English Language*, 1828.

This type of "repentance" shows a lack of a holy fear or respect of God. Proverbs 1:7 says, "The fear of the Lord is the beginning of knowledge, but fools despise wisdom and discipline." This is not an isolated scripture. Numerous scriptures talk about the fear of the Lord as a good and holy reverence. This fear is not the kind spoken of in 1 John 4:18, which states, "There is no fear in love. But perfect love drives out fear, because fear has to do with punishment. The man who fears is not made perfect in love."

Experiencing God's love drives the wrong kind of fear out of our lives. Eradicating that fear is good and critically needed. But the fear spoken of in Proverbs 1:7 is different. It's a deep, holy respect and awe of God. It is a realization that there are consequences for wrongdoing and disobeying God. It motivates us to keep away from those things that are wrong for us.

Our motivation to want to live a life pleasing to God should primarily be love for Him. But a Christian should also have a holy awe of God, and a knowing that disobeying Him or living our lives contrary to God's Word, the Bible, will have negative consequences.

Believers who do not have a proper respect for God and His Word will live marginal Christian lives, at best. Their doctrine, or belief system, will be partly scriptural and partly based on what the world says is right. They need a change of heart to want to please the Lord in all areas of their lives.

Not because God is standing over us with a big stick to beat us when we do wrong. But because living His way is what is best for us and straying from that will hurt our lives.

Repentance is both wanting our relationship to be right with God, and fleeing from sin and its consequences. Repentance is more than mouthing words asking God to forgive us. It involves sincere regret for any actions or deeds that were sinful or improper.

John the Baptist was sent to prepare Israel, and all else who would listen, to receive Jesus and salvation. His coming ministry was foretold many years earlier, as recorded in John 1: "You will go on before the Lord to prepare the way for him, to give His people the knowledge of salvation through the forgiveness of their sins" (verses 76-77). In fact, the angel Gabriel, in telling of John's coming birth, stated, "He will . . . turn the hearts of the fathers to their children and the disobedient to the wisdom of the righteous- to make ready a people prepared for the Lord" (Luke 1:17)

How did John do this? "He went into all the country around the Jordan, preaching a baptism of repentance for the forgiveness of sins" (Luke 3:3). John proclaimed the need to repent and turn to the Lord to obtain salvation. In addition, men's repentance would lead to the restoration of families by turning "the hearts of the fathers to their children."

When we turn to the Lord with a repentant and open heart, He changes us. That change will lead to a change in priorities, which will involve and bring transformation to our families. This is part of our role as husband and father: God wants us to love, nourish, care for, and protect our families. not just provide for them materially.

True repentance involves a sorrow for the wrong that was done. In 2 Corinthians 7:10 we see that, *"Godly sorrow brings repentance that leads to salvation and leaves no regret, but worldly sorrow brings death."* Godly sorrow is not groveling in the dust, but a sincere regret. The result should be for us to "turn away" from those things we recognize as harmful to our life. Then, we no longer focus on these areas after we come to realize we need to change. We do not live in the past but focus on moving forward with God.

Please remember, *God* does not condemn us. Satan is the accuser of God's people, not God. However, God will convict us and draw us to surrender to Him and change our direction when needed. We experience sorrow when we see the consequences of sin and how it affects us and those around us. When we do, we naturally want to turn away from it and toward God and His ways.

When I was younger, I worked for a difficult man. My boss was bright and determined, but could be very demanding and difficult. He was proud. At times his ego was a bit overwhelming. I was a Christian; my boss wasn't. Admittedly, I too, was driven and didn't like being looked down upon or spoken to in anger. I felt I needed to stand my ground. Sometimes there was real conflict between my boss and me. Looking back, I am surprised he didn't fire me! Thank God, I needed the money to support my family.

One day, I was reading the Book of Colossians. I had read this passage many times before, but it leaped off of the page at me this time:

> *Servants, obey in all things your masters according to the flesh, not with eye service, as men-pleasers, but in sincerity of heart, fearing God. And whatever you do, do it heartily, as to the Lord and not to men, knowing that from the Lord you will receive the reward of the inheritance; for you serve the Lord Christ. But he who does wrong will be repaid for the wrong which he has done, and there is no partiality. (Colossians 3:22-25)*

As I read this, I became convicted regarding my attitude toward my boss. Even though he was difficult, I realized I had shown a lack of respect and did not have a servant's heart toward him. God used His Word to convict me of my own wrong attitudes and actions. I was really tempted to harden my heart! I went to the Lord in prayer and struggled through my own pride and self-justification. In the end, I chose to repent, and with the Lord's help, I determined to change my attitudes. I went to my boss and confessed my wrong attitudes to him and asked for his forgiveness. He didn't know what to say. But after that, our relationship changed for the better.

Ask for Forgiveness

When God brings us to repentance, we will not only need to ask the Lord's forgiveness, we will often need to go to others and ask their forgiveness. Matthew 5:263-24 says, *"Therefore, if you are offering your gift at the altar and there remember that your brother has something against you, leave your gift there in front of the altar. First go and be reconciled to your brother; then come and offer your gift."* Clearly, the Lord wants us to clear up problems in our relationships.

When we become aware that we have offended another person, we are to go to them and confess the wrong we have done and ask forgiveness. We may feel that the other person was also at fault, or that the problem is at least some percentage their fault. However, this is not a game of keeping score or figuring percentages. Our responsibility is to do what God requires of us.

The key here is to be clean before God. David said:

> *Cleanse me with hyssop, and I will be clean; wash me, and I will be whiter than snow. Let me hear joy and gladness; let the bones you have crushed rejoice. Hide your face from my sins and blot out all my iniquity. Create in me a pure heart, O God, and renew a steadfast spirit within me. Do not cast me from your presence or take your Holy Spirit from me. Restore to me the joy of your salvation and grant me a willing spirit, to sustain me. (Psalms 51:7-12)*

We are to cleanse ourselves by obeying the leading and promptings of the Holy Spirit. We are responsible for ourselves; God is responsible for others. Our responsibility is to humble ourselves and go to others, when appropriate, and ask forgiveness. If they in turn ask for forgiveness, then the relationship has been reestablished. However, we must go with the expectation that they will offer no apology in return. Our biblical responsibility is to fulfill what the Lord would have us to do, whether or not others feel they have done any wrong.

Simply be obedient. Do as the Lord is prompting you and be free. I also encourage you to approach this time prayerfully, and ask God to help you. Ask Him to grant you the humility to do this properly. Also ask for favor and for the other person to have an open heart. We want the relationship to be restored, if appropriate, and forgiveness granted.

Asking for forgiveness does not begin with, "If I have done anything to hurt or offend you. . ." When we ask for forgiveness, we admit what we did wrong and ask the other person to forgive us. There is no "if." We also do not bring up the other person's offense. We take responsibility for our actions.

We should ask for forgiveness with sincerity (e.g., "I'm sorry if I offended you."). We did hurt or offend them; that's why we're asking forgiveness. If the other person detects a lack of sincerity, they may *say* they forgive you, but they may sense there is no true remorse. True forgiveness has not been asked nor granted.

In my life, there have been many times I have been convicted of offending or wronging another in some way. I have gone to a number of people over the years and asked forgiveness for my actions, words, or attitudes. But there have been many times I felt others should have come to ask my forgiveness, even Christians, and they did not. That's okay. I must do what is right before the Lord.

After God convicted me of my attitudes toward my boss, I went to him, confessed my bad attitudes, and asked for forgiveness. My boss was taken back. However, he accepted my apology. From that time, I tried to be the best worker and employee I could. My attitude changed toward my boss, and our relationship changed dramatically. His confidence in me grew, along with his trust, and he began to entrust me with more responsibility. There was also a change in his attitude toward me. We became friends.

Our responsibility is to seek forgiveness when we know we've wronged someone. If they in turn ask forgiveness for their actions or attitudes, that is a real and unexpected bonus that can lead to a much deeper relationship between them and you. You may be surprised at what God will do!

Make Restitution

Asking forgiveness of the Lord is the first step in mending relationships. But we must be prepared to confess it to others when appropriate and make restitution—or "make it right," if needed, as well as ask for forgiveness.

Chad worked in a small retail store when he was a teenager. While there, he discovered it was easy to steal money from the cash register. Over the next two years, he took money each time he worked. Years later, he gave his heart to Christ. During prayer one day, the Holy Spirit began to convict him of his actions. He called the owner, confessed his actions, and committed to paying the money back. It took him several years of making payments, but he finally paid it back.

Chad not only asked for forgiveness, he went the next step of making it right. Restitution means "to restore what was lost." Webster defines this as: "The act of making good, or of giving the equivalent for any loss, damage, or injury; restoring to someone some thing, or right of which he has been unjustly deprived."

If we have stolen, we should pay it back if we can. The other party may forgive us and release us from the debt, but we have to be prepared for the fact that they may not. Either way, we need to do what is right.

Restitution can be made in material goods, restoring a reputation, establishing the truth, and so on. It may involve more than one person. As a general rule, the request for forgiveness and the offer/action of restitution should be as broad as the original offense, when possible. If you have gossiped or soiled the reputation of another, you will need to go to those you gossiped to and confess your wrong and ask for their forgiveness.

This happened to me many years ago, when I was an elder in a church. I was relatively young and very zealous for the Lord. A problem began to arise in the church regarding the pastor; a number of people on the leadership team—myself included—were losing confidence in him.

I felt a need to fix the problem. My relationships with many of the church leaders went back a number of years, and I was sensitive to their feelings as well as my own. I called a meeting of the church leaders and announced that I thought the pastor needed to be replaced. Most of the other leaders agreed and followed my leadership. The result was a church split, in which many of the leadership team, and my family and I, left the church.

A year later, during a time I had set aside for prayer and fasting, the Lord began to convict me of my actions. I realized I had not sought the Lord about what to do regarding the problem in the church. I had reacted, and had taken a course of action that seemed right at the time. But I had not sought God's wisdom or direction. I had also betrayed the pastor who had trusted me. The

Lord convicted me that I was to go to that pastor and ask forgiveness for my actions and the resulting church split.

I also recognized I had to call all of the past church leaders and confess my failure; that I had led them into an action that resulted in the church split. I had been sincere—but sincerely wrong. What I should have done was call the leadership team into prayer and fasting, and tried to mend the problem, not cause a tear in relationships.

The following Sunday, I went to that church and confessed to the pastor. I also asked if I could address the whole church. I stood before the entire congregation and confessed my wrongdoing and asked for forgiveness.

Afterwards, many men gathered around me, extending forgiveness and affirmation. Our fellowship was restored! The pastor, too, forgave me and expressed his desire for me and my family to return to the church.

The point I want to make here is that while I (rightly) asked God to forgive me, there was more at stake than just myself. I had been entrusted with the position of an elder in the church. That trust carried responsibility to the church. Since my offense affected the entire church, I believed the restitution had to be made to the entire church and its past leaders. That was a difficult action, but one that bore much fruit in my life and in the life of others. A load was lifted and fellowship restored.

A Life Marked by Forgiveness

Whether we are the ones who have wronged or others have wronged us, we want to be like God in our actions and responses. Since He stands ready to forgive everyone who repents and turns to Him, He wants us to show mercy and forgive others.

We do not lose our salvation due to unforgiveness, but we do live with its consequences. We can be in a "prison," living with all of the negative feelings, emotions, anger, and other problems that come due to unforgiveness. The Lord wants us to be free. He came that we might live life "abundantly," not be bound or hindered in life.

How can we understand God's love until we understand His forgiveness and mercy? How can we understand His grace toward us until we have practiced it toward others?

Until we have loved, how can we understand love, especially God's love? Until we have forgiven, how can we understand how God forgives and loves us? Until we practice love, forgiveness and extending grace toward others, we cannot experience it for ourselves as God intends.

The really great thing is that God is there to help us do this. As we ask Him to help us and decide to obey Him, His Spirit goes to work giving us grace to forgive others. Think of this: obeying God brings greater grace to us. We then become His channel to release His grace to others.

QUESTIONS FOR REFLECTION AND DISCUSSION

1. Are you aware of someone you have harmed or offended? If so, whom? How did you offend that person? (Note: If you have a tendency to recall every wrong thing you have ever done, ask God to help you discern which offenses He would have you focus on.)

   _____
   _____
   _____
   _____

ASKING FORGIVENESS AND MAKING RESTITUTION

2. Have you confessed the offense and asked the person for forgiveness? If so, what was the result? If not, is that a step you are willing to take?

　_____
　_____
　_____
　_____

3. Were there any Scripture passages in the lesson, or the ones preceding it, that stood out to you? Which one(s)? What is God saying to you through His Word?

　_____
　_____
　_____
　_____

4. Do you need to make restitution for this harm or offense in some way? If so, how?

　_____
　_____
　_____
　_____

TAKE A KNEE

Let's pray. *"Dear Father. I want to have the holy fear of You the Bible says I should have. I desperately need to know and experience Your love for me, the love that casts out fear of all I should not be afraid of. Help me to have the proper awe and respect of You. I ask You, Holy Spirit, to bring this to pass in my life.*

"Father, please reveal to me any I have offended whom I need to ask for forgiveness, that I may be free in those areas and my heart will be right before you. Also, please show me if I need to make restitution. I want to clear up any problems with any relationships that exist. Give me the strength, the humility, and the resolve to do this."

A FINAL WORD

Christ died for us all. He values us all. He values our relationship not only with Him, but with each other.

Failing to forgive others can have far-reaching effects in our lives, including affecting our relationship with God and others. God wants us to be free of unforgiveness, hurt, anger, or other negative emotions that can plague us. He wants us to live in freedom. His joy and peace are more important than choosing to take up offenses with others. Forgive others! Be free!

In addition, God wants us to have a holy fear of Him. This healthy reverence compels us to flee from sin and its consequences. It should motivate us to want to serve Him and learn His ways, so we will strive to live a righteous life. It should also cause us to want to restore any relationships that need to be restored. He is our righteousness. He wants to live out His life in us. He desires to remove any obstacles that would prevent that from happening. He does this in love, with patience, and through His grace toward us. God loves us! God is good!

ABOUT THE AUTHOR

Lou Turner wrote *Living Life God's Way* out of his passion for men to discover God, and to get to know Him and what He has for them. This 13-book men's discipleship series is the culmination of Lou's own journey—a life of seeking God, studying His Word, memorizing Scripture and meditating on it, and practical experience with family, community, marketplace work, and Christian ministry. It also comes, by Lou's own admission, from life experiences of both successes and mistakes, as a result of both good and bad decisions.

Lou has headed ministries, written and taught workshops, classes, and seminars, and discipled dozens of men. Now, he has put into print the things he has learned to help other men along their path and journey.

Most of Lou's growing up years were spent in Detroit and its suburbs, where he was raised in a pastor's home. Following his graduation from university with a Bachelor of Science in Business Administration, Lou and his wife planted and pastored a church for three years. After that time, he felt the strong call of God to return to business.

Over the years, Lou has served in numerous senior executive positions with national and international companies in the real estate and oil and gas industries. As of this writing, Lou is still active in business with his own home building company. He has

ABOUT THE AUTHOR

been married to his wife Joan since they were 20. They have three children and 10 grandchildren and make their home in Phoenix, Arizona.

www.ingramcontent.com/pod-product-compliance
Lightning Source LLC
Chambersburg PA
CBHW021124080526
44587CB00010B/628